MW01136856

Slithering Snakes
Boomslangs

by Julie Murray

Dash!
LEVELED READERS

1

Dash!

LEVELED READERS

Level 1 – Beginning
Short and simple sentences with familiar words or patterns for children who are beginning to understand how letters and sounds go together.

Level 2 – Emerging
Longer words and sentences with more complex language patterns for readers who are practicing common words and letter sounds.

Level 3 – Transitional
More developed language and vocabulary for readers who are becoming more independent.

abdopublishing.com

Published by Abdo Zoom, a division of ABDO, P.O. Box 398166, Minneapolis, Minnesota 55439.
Copyright © 2018 by Abdo Consulting Group, Inc. International copyrights reserved in all countries.
No part of this book may be reproduced in any form without written permission from the publisher.

Printed in the United States of America, North Mankato, Minnesota.
092017
012018

Photo Credits: Alamy, iStock, National Geographic Creative, Shutterstock, Superstock
Production Contributors: Kenny Abdo, Jennie Forsberg, Grace Hansen, John Hansen
Design Contributors: Dorothy Toth, Neil Klinepier

Publisher's Cataloging in Publication Data

Names: Murray, Julie, author.
Title: Boomslangs / by Julie Murray.
Description: Minneapolis, Minnesota: Abdo Zoom, 2018. | Series: Slithering snakes |
    Includes online resource and index.
Identifiers: LCCN 2017939242 | ISBN 9781532120725 (lib.bdg.) | ISBN 9781532121845 (ebook) |
    ISBN 9781532122408 (Read-to-Me ebook)
Subjects: LCSH: Boomslangs--Juvenile literature. | Snakes--Juvenile literature. | Reptiles--Juvenile
    literature.
Classification: DDC 597.96--dc23
LC record available at https://lccn.loc.gov/2017939242

Table of Contents

Boomslangs

Boomslangs are dangerous snakes. They can be deadly!

They are found in Africa.
They mainly live in trees.

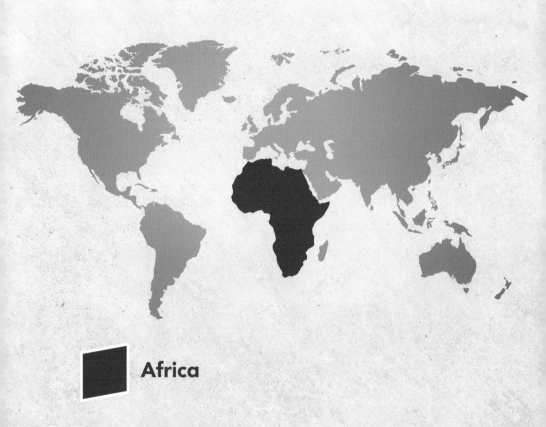

Africa

They have two **fangs**. Their fangs release **venom**.

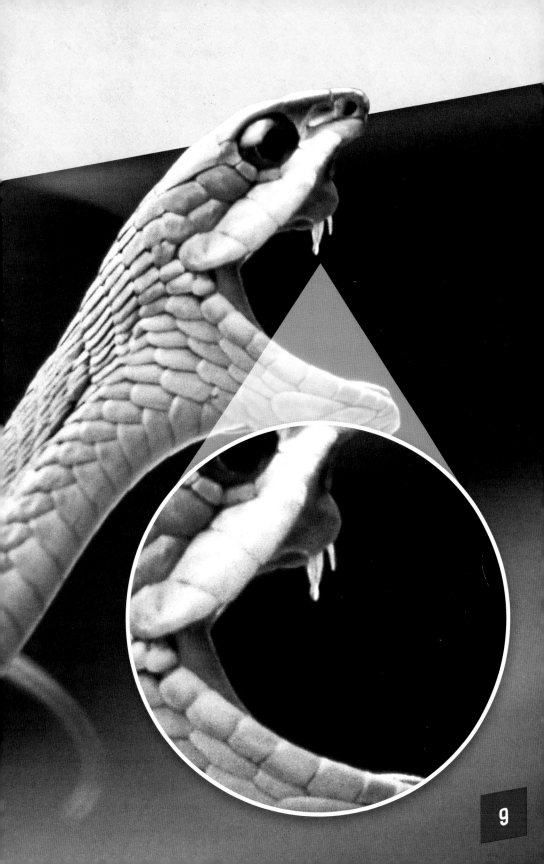

Their **fangs** are in the back of their mouth.

They eat birds and lizards.

They also eat small **mammals**.

Many are green in color.
Some are brown or gray.

They have two large eyes. They have **excellent** eyesight!

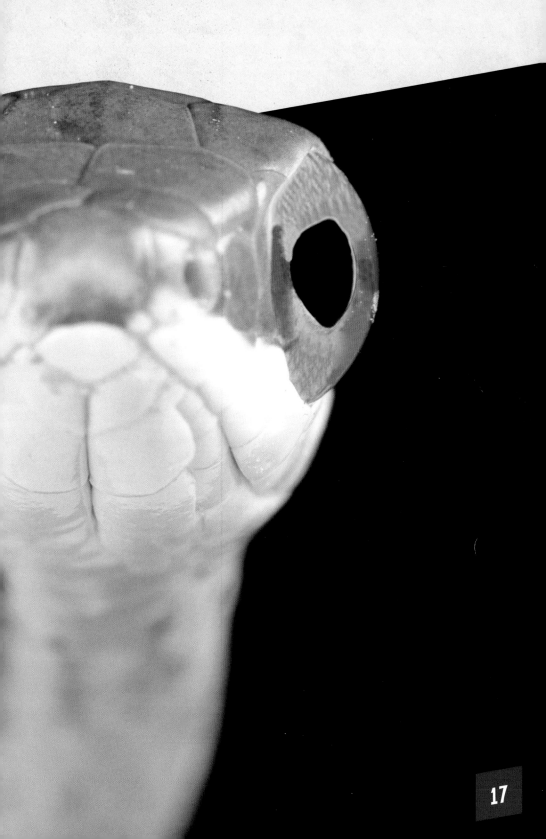

Boomslangs are thin.
They can be 4 to 6
feet (1.2-1.8 m) long.

They can live for 8
years in the wild.

More Facts

- Boomslang means "tree snake" in **Afrikaans**.

- They can open their mouths 170 degrees.

- Their **fangs** are small. They are only 3–5mm (1/8–3/16 inches) long.

Glossary

Afrikaans – a language spoken in South Africa.

excellent – very good or much better than others.

fang – a long, pointed tooth that is used to bite prey and inject venom.

mammal – a warm-blooded animal with fur or hair on its skin and a skeleton inside its body.

venom – the poison that certain snakes produce.

Index

Online Resources

Booklinks
NONFICTION NETWORK
FREE! ONLINE NONFICTION RESOURCES

To learn more about boomslangs, please visit **abdobooklinks.com**. These links are routinely monitored and updated to provide the most current information available.